ANCHOR
BOOKS

ANCHOR POETS AROUND BRITAIN 1999

Edited by

Heather Killingray

First published in Great Britain in 1999 by
ANCHOR BOOKS
1-2 Wainman Road, Woodston,
Peterborough, PE2 7BU
Telephone (01733) 230761

HB ISBN 1 85930 697 7
SB ISBN 1 85930 692 6

FOREWORD

Anchor Books is a small press, established in 1992, with the aim of promoting readable poetry to as wide an audience as possible.

We hope to establish an outlet for writers of poetry who may have struggled to see their work in print.

The poems presented here have been selected from many entries. Editing proved to be a difficult task and as the Editor, the final selection was mine.

I trust this selection will delight and please the authors and all those who enjoy reading poetry.

Heather Killingray
Editor

CONTENTS

Thoughts

The expectation of life for men
Is three score years and ten.
Some have more and some have less
If you reach seventy! That's success.
But when you have reached that sell-by date,
Deterioration, that's your fate.
A check up on your teeth is due,
Fillings, extractions, dentures too.
You cannot see without your glasses.
You've forgotten the time when men made passes
At pretty girls. Now heavy sighs
Replace the winks of laughing eyes,
Devouring sights of mini-skirts
The flash of thighs . . . Oh, how it hurts!

Norma Marshman

LORD TELL ME WHY!

A petal drops - a leaf falls,
The sunsets with fading shadows on the walls,
Worms and insects are swallowed after chicks hungry demanding calls,
They're fighting to live, to survive, yet the inevitable end,
Everyone and everything deliberately stalls.

Lord Tell Me Why!

Seas and rivers welcome residents and visitors with ever open arms,
Caressing all creatures and plants with their unceasingly flowing
charms,
Who bravely journey through floods and droughts, raging storms or
becalms,
Only to be either eaten, hooked or washed up next to Caribbean palms.

Lord Tell Me Why!

Lapwing, gull, sparrow, finch, hawk or tit,
Thermal filled skies above earth they all and others fit.
The elements they endure with remarkable stamina and grit,
Alas sometimes to perish, to starve, in turn they all eventually quit.

Lord Tell Me Why!

We're born, we breath, we see, we hear,
We walk, talk, touch, gifts we all hold dear
We strive and struggle with deep feelings of love, happiness of joy,
despair or fear,
Thus preparing us for lives twisting winding course we all
independently steer.
Until one day our journeys end unavoidably grows near,
And then and only then the answer to my recurring question now
becomes clear.

Lord Tell Me Why!

Tina Davenport

THE SONG OF WANDERING AUTOLYCUS

(Air: The Streams of Bunclody.)

O were we on the mailboat and could see the Hill of Howth
It would put a new song in my brazen biddy's mouth:
It is drinking of bad liquor makes her tongue to revile,
And the strong Saxon bridewell is within but half a mile.

Come all you little streamers, and weep like the dew;
Did she ask to be born, or be twisted as she grew?
Now she lies at my feet, disarrayed by her fall,
More stocious than Tandy in the bay of Donegal.

If I were a fiddler and could tune a pretty string
I'd recall her lost beauty and set men marvelling
But I am a deaf beggar beyond whose grasp it lies -
O Raftery, dark Raftery, has God yet given you eyes?

Since my own tongue is weak to do justice to her pain
I will go to some dead master and steal his refrain;
I will thank Maurice Craig that taught the trick to me -
O Ferriter, Piers Ferriter, how blooms your gallows tree?

She was once as brave a colleen for whom to march and die
As might evoke the gun-peal and wake the slogan-cry,
And were we on the mail-boat, a-breasting of the Kish,
You should see her transfigured, as fair as man could wish.

For the shattered night-walker a sword bars the way:
She will never pass Caergybi, and with her I must stay,
Thinking long on harp-and heart-strings that had played a gracious tune
If it hadn't been for the Porter's froth and the yellow river's moon. . .

I am an old beggar that has watched a deal of wrong,
And the seer of Ben Bulben may fitly end my song:
As he wrote upon the wreckage of an earlier, bitter day;
O what of that, O what of that, what is there left to say?

Christopher Monro

O'Malley's Dream

On Conemara mountain
I met a pretty fellow.
His hair was the brightest pink
One eye blue
The other yellow!

On Connemara mountain
One bright and sunny morn.
I met a funny creature
They call the unicorn!

On Connemara mountain
A man never grows too old.
O'Hagan tells this to me
The tale as he was told!

On Connemara mountain
Day and night are always sunny.
No leaves grow upon the trees
Just loads, me boys, of money!

On Connemara mountain
Gold pieces are a chinkin.
And the fiddler plays a love song
To the life force we are drinkin!

Should you wish view it
Friend
Search no mountain pass
Look and you will find it
Through the bottom
Of a glass!

T F White

CRUELTY

(With Compliments to Shakespeare's 66th Sonnet)

From these would we be gone: the mixing with
Embattled people who no troth do plight,
With softly sparkling fountain's dew in sunny
Mornings after safe night's caressing dreams.
From bleak Authority's cold hand which clasps
The whip of discord in flailiing ignorance
While meek merit bows in humble stance,
Or the hand withholds from striking when the
Law is but an ass and so would penalise.
From butchers' knives glinting sharply that rend
The heart with gloating fevered avarice,
While anger stumbles in helpless hunger.
From jealousy's pronged tongue that wilfully
Exploits our insecurity to poison
The jewelled goddess of golden virtue.
From statesmen's crafty graft that harnesses
Political intrigue to clutching frozen
Selfishness like wasps in anger stinging
To wake a world to war from troubled sleep.

From these would we be gone to sunnier systems
Except we must await the cruellest joke of all -
The Maker's grinning insolence beneath the pall.

Desmond Tarrant

Table For Two

The table is set for two - I see,
Does that mean just you and me!
I had no intention of coming by
I knew not how the land would lie.

Last week was it Jim, Ian or Fred
Did you take them all to bed?
Or were you waiting just for me
Never mind - we'll just have tea!

Phyllis Wright

PRECIOUS GIFTS

If we had to pay for our freedom
We would spend all we had to be free.
If we had to buy our sight and sound
We would buy it willingly.

If we had to buy a ticket
To smell the beautiful flowers
I am sure that for one scented second
We would all queue up for hours.

If we had to pay to stand on the beach
To breathe in the natural sea air
Or to look at inspiring coastal views
We would go without food just to be there.

Yet none of these things we have to do
They are given to us all old and young
Let us enjoy and appreciate these precious gifts
All free . . . yet priceless to everyone!

Devina Symes

LAST RITES

Commit me not among forgotten graves
But cast my ashes seawards to the waves
Then when you wander barefoot on the shore
I shall return to kiss your feet once more.

Neil Begg

THE SWEETEST LOVE

If I ask
For my heart's desire,
I will have no more
Than I require:
My husband, my children,
My home and my health -
This is the substance of my wealth.

If I tell
What my heart desires,
I can say
'No more than it requires':
All that I am,
And all that is mine
I owe to a love unchanged by time.

Diane Antoniazzi

Garden Gossip

Beans ain't setting, Mr Brown,
Rain we had didn't go down!
Could do with a week's good soak
Otherwise digging will be no joke!

Earth has just got much too dry
Same as you said, Mr Fry.
Carrots haven't moved an inch,
Might get a few beetroot, at a pinch!

Tatties are like marbles too -
Shame - after all the work we do!
Hope cabbage plants do better,
Might do if we get it wetter.

Apples be poor, Mr Brown;
Got good rhubarb off that crown.
Better flavour and quite sweet,
Missus cooks it a real treat!

One good thing, there's no greenfly
That's a blessing, Mr Fry.
Gobbled up by ladybirds,
They do enjoy 'em, so I've heard!

Packing up now, Mr Brown
Cuppa tea, and nice sit down.
'Till tomorrow, Mr Fry.
Forecast says 'tis going to be dry!

Joyce Reeves Holloway

BLACKBERRIES

Some say they are not fit for a suburban plot;
They should be fiercely wrenched out from the clinging soil,
The roots deep dug, then the offensive whole fire-purged.
But on the bank behind the shed they grow luxuriant.
Shyly, first flowers hint at forbidden fruit to come;
Next rigid berries, green, unappetising, stand guard
Against impatient prowling predators, too keen
For early searching forays behind the prickled stems.
Then, overnight it seems, ripe treasure tempts all comers
Seductively to taste the feast; old friends delight
To share the jet black harvest and remembrance springs
Of former childhood wanderings round fragrant hedgerows,
Gleaning rich spoils into a multitude of jars,
With unsuspected sweetness for our autumn days.

Iris Smith

LACUNA

(In Memory Of James Graham RAF
KIA April 1944 Aged 21)

There is a place that's empty still
And will be till I die.
A nagging, aching void
That deepens as years go by.

A father's love and memories sweet
Should that special place have filled,
The way he looked and smiled and spoke
And played with me, his child.

Brothers and sisters there might have been,
Family holidays by the sea.
Christmases we should have shared,
Gathered around the tree.

And on the happiest of days,
His heart a fountain of pride,
He should have walked me down the aisle
To be at my bridegroom's side.

In later years he would have held
My children on his knee,
And smiled and laughed and played with them
As once he did with me.

Instead he lies in a Belgian field,
A madman put him there.
He set the world on fire and killed
The brave, the young, the fair.

They call them 'the glorious dead'
And with pride their names recall,
But where's the glory in death
When on children the sorrows fall?

Patricia Smith

Sadness

When I feel sad I feel an inner silence.
When I feel sad all my hope leaves me and bleakness takes its place.
When I feel sad all I see is blackness and pain.
When I feel sad my smile deserts me.

When I feel sad I recoil inside myself.
When I feel sad all my faith leaves me and misery takes its place.
When I feel sad all I see is despair and frustration.
When I feel sad my fun-loving nature evaporates.

Ekua Ansah-Boateng (14)

SCIENCE IN MY VIEW

The wheel, the catapult, ballistic missiles.
Thundering horses, the saddle, the bit.
Pullinger's humane mousetrap,
Rodents which sent you up the wall, caught very cleverly
by what became known as a 'pitfall'.
Stephenson's 'Rocket', a rage of steam and power
making him 'Man of the Hour'.
Then came the combustion engine,
sending us spinning in all directions
and covering the countryside with grime.
Kittyhawk has a lot to answer for, and yet,
how glorious to soar up to the clouds, imitating birds
and reaching the other end of the world in hours.
Trains roar by, the Chunnel beckons,
destinations reached in seconds.
Central heating, radio, TV.
The Silver Screen, Charlie and BB.
Rockets to the moon and beyond, Mars, the red planet of war.
The glories of Jupiter that Holst saw, in musical form.
Great sea-going liners, and submarines.
Medical breakthroughs and radar beams.
It seems to me science is like a giant switchback,
Tossing the world's population this way and that.
I'd like to believe it's a friend to Mankind . . .
But then I don't have a scientific mind.

Ellsie Russell

A Derbyshire Day

It was magical down by the river,
On a fine hot summer's day.
The air was still and thickly scented
As we ambled on our way.
Suddenly, insects rose in clouds,
Buzzing around in rings,
To settle again when we were past,
Resting singing wings.
Water idled in liquid pools,
Fed by tiny streams,
And further on the water glowed
From light to dark, dark greens.
Rushes and grasses flourished,
Which winter's flow would hide.
And tiny tumbling water bugs
Danced their darting glide.
Jewelled blue-green dragonflies
With transparent, silver wings,
Chased around in coloured bursts
Of exotic shimmerings.
Attuned to nature, seeing, hearing,
Under the shade of leafy trees.
Touching long soft waving grasses,
There to rest - and take our ease.
Being and belonging was enough
As we rested peacefully.
Replete, refreshed, we journeyed home,
These gifts accepting gratefully.

Audrey Clifton

THOUGHTS . . .

A seed that grows to be alive,
With arms, two legs and a smiling face.
A point it reaches, a change, to stop.
No more laughs, but thinks and cries.

Alone and vulnerable, his thoughts spin round.
Do you love? Or, are you loved?
Am I allowed to be just me?
Or must I follow all of Thee?

A boot filled with human extremes
Pushed down and prints a face.
Moulding with your rights and wrongs.
A system to follow with no breaking free.

A shell that looks correct and happy.
Slowly breaks and cracks the rigid edges
Which only a genuine caring touch can do.
You see an image that needs to speak.

'Where am I supposed to be?
Who am I meant to be?
What will the future hold for me?
And, will there always be somebody there for me?'

Rachel Ward

ALONG THE STREAM

Gracefully glide the swans in the stream
Leaving whirlpools where they have been
Further along are moorhens at play
Nose-diving for food then flying away
Seagulls drift amongst them all or
Sometimes watch from a nearby wall
On the surface tiny bubbles appear
The fish below in constant fear
Knowing the birds are hanging about
Just to catch the fishes out.

Eileen Shanley

HARVEST TIME

Harvest time is nearly here
It comes every year
We are the harvest
Of God's good earth
Like corn we grow
From our birth
Some of us fall along the way
With things that we do or say
But as we grow from our youth
We learn to live in love and truth
Forgiving our fellow man
And to help all we can
We are part of God's great plan
The brotherhood of man
One day we all will live in peace
All wars and suffering will cease
Till then we'll plant the seeds of love
Nurtured by the one above.

Sheila Chimes

Six Years Old

I'm crouching, very small,
surrounded by large distortions
to my inner life.
I don't understand
but my self-communion
has been interrupted
and I feel afraid.
Maybe we escaped
to go ponding,
to go to church,
or read a book together.
A good childhood,
most of it secure and loving.
But the air was jagged
and Dad's eyes were hurting
and his inner life
must have felt like mine.
At times I think he understood
and I did not.

Linda J Williams

Regeneration

Cold reflections of the moon
crashing on the sea-carved shore.
Recollections
The voices of our youth,
doomed to die before they are old.
Sentenced by Neptune's trident,
signed and sealed upon the rocks.
Deaf to their mother's cries,
remote from death's sting
haloed upon the wet, cold drifting sand.
'Never!'
Their cries unheard,
buried on an empty wind
deep within their mother's womb.

Duncan Rory Grant

Come, Let Us Hold This Moment

Come, let us hold this moment in our hands,
Shut out the world and its attendant woes.
Live with this hour, forget the unhappy past;
Think not on the future and our changing moods.
Listen! I can hear the beating of your heart.

Outside the wind is blowing wild, tearing the leaves from the trees.
We might ourselves have been those sorry leaves
But here we possess each the other utterly.
Let us hold, enjoy, enrich this hour of ours.
Between us we have the power to do these things.

Another day all might be gone,
You might care no more,
War or circumstance kill the chance.
But come now. Tell me your secret
Within my arms.

Paul Windham Gardner

THE SEASONS OF LIFE

To seek life's changing seasons
through the mists of sombre dawn,
is to watch a flower open
and find an orchid born.

Each show of summer roses
seem more splendid in their prime,
their transience more fleeting,
their grandeur more sublime.

Autumnal breath encroaches,
its jewels of burnished gold
a vestige of the summer's heat,
to have is still to hold.

And the ambience of winter
has its own endearing spell,
the bracing air reviving
before the chiming of the bell.

New life of spring approaches,
its beauty to offset the bleak;
life enhanced is life renewed,
each moment precious and unique.

Yet, soon the evening's mellow glow
will reach the edge of earthly sound,
as our shadows lengthen out of sight
to meet the dust, where stars abound.

Susan Turner

The Eyes Of A Child

I look into the eyes of a child
and see his soul
battered and bruised by inhumanity,
brought to the edge of despair
by ignorance and indifference.

I look into the eyes of a child
and see his hurt;
wounds inflicted by a thoughtless world
have left the aching scars
which cannot be obliterated.

I look into the eyes of a child
and see his tears,
his painful, silent tears as yet unshed,
but time will bring the weeping
with the passing of the years.

I look into the eyes of a child
and see his death,
that numbing death which has preceded mine,
yet he will live in desperate hopelessness
long after I have gone.

Loveday Harmer

On Being Asked To Advise

You ask me to advise you;
My refusal will surprise you,
But I have not been to college
and experience's knowledge
Is not gained by any youngster in an hour.
- Ask me then tomorrow, - by and by -
For the fruit of time will ripen
Like a fruit tree in the garden
In the autumn of its season
When the harvest things are given - by and by.
'Tis then, when toil has taken
What the bloom of youth's forsaken
And time has laid its finger on your soul;
And sorrow may 'a' dimmed you.
But has laid a crown of wisdom over all,
- Ask me then tomorrow, by and by:
'Tis then, if you'll believe me -
And if you will receive me -
I can advise you truly -
I will advise you truly, by and by.
- I'll have lived a little longer
And experience be stronger - by and by.

Verity E S Dibben

PERFECT

Staring into perfect eyes,
Trembling, I start to cry.
I want to be with her,
To hold her near.
To feel her anger, and her fears,
To hold her, touch her, kiss her,
Feel the warmth of her.
Be with her, near her, in her,
And I fall deeper, deeper,
Into love with her.
I dream of a wedding,
In a church by the lake,
I want to give her children,
And maybe we can make,
Perfect harmony.

But maybe not I fear,
The illusions disappear,
For she is never here,
And never will be.
Except for in my dreams,
My perfect fantasies.

Gary Poulton

Snow On Roses

(Christmas '95)

Incredibly, roses blooming in December
Delicately defying rime, reason, time and season;
Granted, not so plush as in their first flush,
Somewhat ragged and faded round the edges
(And their hearts may not really be in it)
But glowing in the steely midwinter morning
Like the previous evening's blood-orange sun.

Now the sky is piled high with meringue
And the candied-peel roses are iced with snow,
Like the slashed sleeve of a Tudor gown,
Crescents of white stuff show against coppery damask.
Above a ground of freezing lace, the searing
Spirit of Christmas Yet-to-Come scythes
Into the lingering attar of summer . . .

Five days later, and the blight was gone;
Incredibly, roses were still blooming in December.

N J Quest

PHILIP

The dreams I've had, the dreams with you,
The dreams that finally came true,
That smile of yours that melts my heart,
The dreams I have when we're apart.

The happy thoughts you bring to me,
Of special things we do and see,
Of days gone by and days to come,
The gleam of something not yet done.

The things I love about you most,
The way you laugh, the way you joke,
The way you're always there for me
Your gentle touch, you kissing me.
The way you hold me close to you,
The way you simply are - just you.

The fire that burns within my heart
Burns more and more as time departs,
You hold the key to slip inside,
To unlock passion, heart and mind.

The love I've held for you so long
Can anyone else feel as strong?
The need to be with you alone,
To hold you tight, to take you home.

To take you in my arms and say,
I love you so much more each day,
This love I know will always last,
You are my present, future, past.

I know that words don't mean that much,
But these are words my heart has touched,
You know you mean the world to me,
I hope your future's here with me.

Virginia Withers

Kiss O' The Dead

I feel the chill of the night but it bothers me not,
the adrenaline inside me makes me feel hot.
I stretch my muscles, for I've been asleep all day.
It seems strange to others but it's my way.

I stand aloft, looking down on the city.
I see the suffering, and I feel pity,
I was once a member of their race,
I shared the sorrow they wear on their face.

But I am no longer a part of their humanity.
The price for this being my own sanity,
I'm driven crazy by the hunger inside.
For me, there's nowhere to hide.

No longer are my eyes a subtle blue,
that used to gently stare at you,
Glowing fierce, a deep crimson red,
they are now the eyes of the Dead.

For I am eternal, and will never die.
Believe what I say as I do not lie,
That despite being a fiend without fear,
every time I feed, I shed a tear.

As I stand with you, discussing my fate,
I can feel my teeth begin to elongate,
They become pointed, as sharp as a pin.
More effective for piercing the skin.

My head pounds, feels ready to burst.
I need your blood to quench my thirst,
I do not kill for deliberate gain,
I only do it to stop the pain.

I feel remorse about my very essence.
I feel guilty and ashamed in your presence,
For I will love you for the rest of eternity,
which is why I do this with some uncertainty.

But I am a vampire and have only one need,
and that is to kill so that I can feed,
I need the sweet, sweet taste of your blood,
which will flow from your neck, in a flood.

As my teeth sink deeper into your veins,
I am released and allowed to forget my pains,
But there is one thought recurring in my head,
and that is that you're being kissed by the Dead.

Antony Putt

Dew

Its very nature
a sodden silk sheet
of love and silence.
The descended, blended
guardian of dawn
gathers her jewels
to nourish the
sod, honour its God
and still complete
appears to pay
nature its due.

T Noel Davies

THE MACHINIST

I applied for a job in a factory,
When I was fourteen years old,
'You'll learn how to sew, and make dresses,
And have a good trade', I was told!

I arrived with tape measure and scissors,
And a 'pinny' to keep myself clean,
Then was led to a very large workroom,
To learn how to use a machine.

There were three other girls, I remember,
Who started the same day as me,
And we struck up a very good friendship,
On that we all had to agree.

One day, every summer, the factory would close,
And we'd climb into the buses outside,
With bags full of sweets, we'd sit back in our seats,
And settle ourselves for the ride.

As the bus travelled on, through the long country lanes,
Taking us down to the sea,
We'd sing and we'd laugh, and not think about work,
Or what the weather would be!

Now I look back, with such sadness,
As the old factory closed long ago,
But I'll always remember with pleasure,
The days when I learnt how to sew.

Hazel Hunt

MILES AWAY

Like thunder the waves leapt against the cliffs,
Gulls screamed as they skimmed above the rocks,
Wildness, yet peace, silence.
He stood and watched, a man all alone.

What was going through his mind?
Was it memories of things gone by?
White spray lurched into the air,
He stood so still, I wonder why.

No motion from his head,
No turning against the wind,
The sea birds circled, looked, and flew away,
Then suddenly he turned to me and grinned.

He raised his hat as he walked past
Still dreaming of the sea,
Into the distant hills he walked,
If he had stayed we could have talked.
Maybe he didn't really notice me!

Jean Tapping

An Observation

Cars full of people
Chase each other
Along the straight grey road.
Watching.
In adjacent field of green,
A sheep twitches one ear
And goes on chewing its cud.

Elizabeth Rainsford

The Fruit Falls

A river of a beech, dark moss
islands on its face,
is flowing to its oasis

of summer emerald, a well
of slow ripening.
Another world is deepening:

its fruit is falling, beating time
on leaf mould's velvet.
The clock of the woods, time's claret

through the shadows, kernels peeping
from their whiskered homes
at new harbours - and my hair thrums

with the breeze that's never sleeping.

Chris White

Retirement

As I sit here in the sunshine
All I can see from my easy chair is mine.
Veg in my garden growing well,
Some for me, extra to sell.
Lawn all mown nice and short,
Grass smells sweet and clean just like it ought.
Sweet fragrance from wallflowers
While I sit here in my chair willing away the hours.
But oh heck!
The sun is burning my neck.
Feet up resting awhile after washing pots up.
Couple of hours then have a sup.
Everything in garden is fine and dandy.
The old easy chair has come in handy.
I wonder why.
Not a cloud in the sky.
Boy it's grand to be retired.
Now my work permit has expired.
For to sit about
Doing nowt.
Enjoy life while I can.
'Cos when health goes life goes down the pan.
Life for me has slowed down for a while,
While I retired and got a pile.

T E Hopkins

TROUBLES SHARED

When you are thinking that nobody cares,
And your heart is broken and you've no one to share,
Put on your walking boots,
Woolly hat and scarf,
Then your troubles will vanish,
Well! At least by half.

Call on your friends and say, 'Let's go' and,
Walk in the sunshine,
Rain, snow or blow.
Hear all their stories,
As you walk along, and
Try to be cheerful,
When they sing you a song.

Listen to the birds, high in the trees,
Breathe in fresh air in the soft morning breeze.
At the end of the day,
When you're tired and worn,
Think of tomorrow,
Then you won't feel forlorn.

Elsie Smith

Memories

I walked in worlds unknown to you,
Thronging crowds under burning sun.
Toiling bodies with sweat and oil,
Burdens too great, back aching toil.
Traffic horns vie with squeaking brakes,
Rickshaw bells tinkle near the kerbside.
Traders and vendors sell their wares,
Sizzling titbits from roadside pans.
With yards of coffee pouring hot
Quench thirst and hunger on the spot.

I walked in worlds unknown to you,
Kashmir valleys and waterfalls.
Snow clad ranges stand sharp and white
Floating gardens by day and night.
Noisy bazaars, burning joss sticks
Midst pictures, carvings of ivory.
Houseboats hug the lakeside pathway,
Bobbing on lapping water.
Slender sari-clad women glide
Beside the lake at eventide.

Sister Gregory

JESUS OUR LORD DIED FOR US

One day, a long time ago,
Jesus Our Lord died
Along with two thieves,
One on either side.

He was born to die
For me and you.
And as He died
The veil was torn in two.

There was darkness around,
The earth began to quake.
The tombs broke open,
The holy people were awake.

Then on the third day He rose
From death to set us free.
We too will rise after death,
To reign with Him eternally.

Doreen Swann

TREASURED MEMORIES

The bells didn't ring in 1945 when Mam and Dad got wed,
but their vows were sincerely honoured when the words were said.
A church on a hilltop is where they made their legal bond,
witnessed by their parents and a few close friends.
Their many years together has now reached fifty one,
fond memories and photos old and new to dwell upon.
They have been blessed with four children, Christine, Margaret
Michael and me,
taught us how to love, respect and have dignity.
Over the years they've both worked hard to maintain our happy life,
from our early childhood, to us finding three husbands and a wife.
We too have been blessed with children of our own,
the notches getting higher to mark how tall they've grown.
We're sure to teach them well before they leave the nest,
our knowledge passed on from parents who are the best.
Our lives are sometimes hectic as we try to pay our way,
work seems overwhelming, no time to rest or play.
But for the time we spend with you, we all treasure every minute,
the love still pouring through, embracing our families within it.
I hope this poem has painted a picture for you all to see
a portrait of a loving couple and a family tree.

Audrey Holmes

THE CITY

People shuffling, scurrying,
Hurrying to and fro,
This way, that way, no way,
Not knowing where to go.

Running, walking, shouting, talking,
Or silent and determined,
Getting nowhere fast,
Simple and yet certain.

Eyes staring without expression,
Some peering with intent,
At others who are passing,
Not knowing where they went.

Ant-like stampeding into shops,
Handling, feeling, buying,
Retreating from the counter,
Satisfied and sighing.

Banging, bumping, racing
To catch bus Number One,
Exhausted, slumping, laden,
Now their work is done.

Denise M Blunt

EQUALITY AND THE BETTER PEOPLE

All are equal - that's a joke.
Blow it out as you would a cigarette's smoke
The better people are way up there
Look around you and you will see them everywhere
Admire their fancy clothes
Or envy them whenever they pass
Among human beings - there's got to be class
Equality where can you be?
Classless society stop hiding from me
Egalitarianism show me your face
Are you ashamed of this poverty-stricken place?
Lift me up - I'm calling on you
Am I among the rejected too?
Capitalism lend a listening ear
Socialism is shrinking from fear
Democracy you're acting very strange
Has honesty and decency gotten your range?
Hypocrisy show your other face
Order dictatorship out of our place
The high-class people make all the laws
We have to feel the sting of their claws.

End

Omald Bakker

SUNFLOWER

Supporting a petal-headed sun on its apex,
this segmented stem taught hairs
to stand perpendicular
and each leaf
had a tough veined heart.

Weight in the seed store bent stalk to buckling point
and leaves were sprinkled with holes.
Irresistible lean began,
the cane was only halfway high.

With a new cane
alongside its full stature,
growth was more certain
for five infant flowers
in leaf clefts below,
also for tuberous roots not designed
to withstand excessive strain.

Chris Antcliff

UNTITLED

(On hearing a second year music student play cello at Nottingham University)

Tall thin talented
Whence
Comes the strength
The cello to play?
A part of your body
It became
Not only today
But for the future
When on the concert platform
You will make your name.
Lauded, applauded,
A future Jacqueline Dupré
Where from comes talent?
Is it instinct?
Is it acquired?
Whichever, it is to be desired.
How dull, how grey
Without it we would be.
Thank you for playing
So soulfully
Encore to eternity.

W B McDade

To Walk With You

I would like to walk with you
Along the ridged sand of a northern beach
With the hiss and roar of the ebb-tide
And the stinging sea spray
Swirling about our ears.

I would like to walk with you
Across a high and windy moor
With tough tentacles of heather tugging at our feet
And ahead of us a grass-grown road
Towards our destination.

I would like to walk with you
In the crowded streets of a town
Surrounded by a heaving sea of strangers
Pushed and pulled by the press of bodies
And your hand fast in mine.

I would like to walk with you
Through the flowering woods in springtime
Along the June hedgerows at evening
Across the singing summer fields
And then to bring you home.

Helen Parsons

The Reunion

They all gathered round on that dismal day,
The wind struck up and the sky turned grey,
'He was a good boy,' I heard someone sigh,
As she pulled out her hanky and started to cry.

But I had no tears left, I had cried them all,
And as the sky darkened the rain began to fall,
Weeping the tears that I couldn't, as if it knew,
What it was to feel the sorrow I felt over you.

Was it only last week you held me in your arms?
It seems like only yesterday, you were so calm
As you walked to your car and kissed me goodbye
And told me to 'be good' and never to cry.

Now I won't see you again, I must start my life anew,
But how I wish I'd been killed in that car crash with you.
The service is now over, people begin to disappear,
An arm is put around me, 'Come along with me, dear.'

Kind people and friends want to start my life again,
Help me try to forget all the sorrow and the pain,
But soon I will join you and leave this awful place.
In the papers next evening there's another suicide case.

Andrea Shepherd

The Cure

At last they come, those blessed healing tears,
That rack the frame and tears the soul apart,
Those frozen tears melt now,
To bathe away,
The searing pain,
That burns within her heart.

Barbara Peters

Tempus Fugit

A thousand years
Is but a day
To our Creator
Wise men say
Two days hath come
Two days hath gone
Since on this earth
He walked upon
He sweeps the sons
Of men away
As quickly as
Night turns to day
As quickly as
Ripe ears of corn
Are mown down
On a summer's morn
A thousand years
A day but just;
When man shall
Turn back into dust.

Mary C Soden

THE BUTTY-CABIN

Jack left number one fly -
for a saunter down Plum Pudding Alley,
glass of grog at The Morning's Pride -
left lace-edged plates, polished brasses
in capable care of his boatwoman wife's
navigable hands. She would have
castle pudding ready on his return.
They would moor up at The Packet Boat,
he'd do a deal with the ex-boatman landlord
over 'backfired' cargo -
'I s'll niver be a scollard like your son!'
he'd say to the taverner's wife,
before returning to his own, like a drunken,
wretched navvy, cursing, demanding his meal.
In-between round-the-clock shifting pounds
and summits, the memory of the tap, he'd hear
butty-boat ballads of doomed heroines,
fairy tales of fluffy roses and firm castles,
bright Phoebe and giant plopping water voles
that scared skittish even circus-trained
boat-horses - and magical stories of stags
in luminant landscapes.

Kenneth Berry

Rosanna's Ride

Rosanna's ride
In dirty waters
Mississippi steamer
Time will leave her
She saw
Sunrise
Shadows crawl
Across her floor
Dauphine Street
Dizzy whore
Southern Belle
Civil war
Jackson Square
A Vanity Fair
Girls work
Southern Comfort

Andrew John Revell

Calm

Languid waters gently swell
Rocking my boat as I lie alone
Entranced by the soothing rhythm
Of waves lapping against the hull

So listless I am this afternoon
Only the faintest breeze in my hair
Wisps of cloud race far above
Through the everlasting azure sky

The sun beats down as I gaze up
Shading my eyes from the burning rays
Blue meets blue from ocean to sky
Joined by a transient shimmering haze

Safe at my anchor here in the bay
I watch the seabirds drift on by
Wheeling like graceful dancers on ice
Masters of their ethereal domain

Time moves on and my mind is blank
Feel like I'm drunk without drinking
Paradise I've found at least for a while
Until the sun starts sinking

Looking back, the thin golden shore
Calls me towards the shady palms
So with a sigh I do withdraw
Now I am rested by this calm

Mark G Ireland

A Sunken Treasure

Sweet bumblebee'd woodbine in love,
grasping in reach for the sun.
Dewy clusters of honeysuckle
attracts Mr B's attention.

Deep velvet dressed he daintily dithers
passionately sipping the fruits.
Busily, buzzingly bobbing the breeze,
diving around twisted roots.

Citrus jasmine creeps beneath the sill,
collecting wasps in perfumed trance.
Camouflaged they whisperingly rest,
'til there's news of a jam pot chance.

Climbing the old rusty brickwork,
pale pink petalled roses entwine.
Dusky meringues set in olive-green silks
hide the greenflies in folds sipping wine.

Peering in the corner
amongst the rocky mossy bed,
in bush shade, in moth's glade they glow.
In leather leaves, lie lily of the valley
miniature bells, a purer white than snow.

Emerald ferns like peacocks proud,
feathered lightly against the grey.
The elder fern is buff and crisp
yet will not fade away.

Forget-me-not they tinkle
Each tiny pale blue star.
Forget thee not, I will never,
a treasured memory for ever
a childhood scar.

MAT

Pop Nostalgia

Do you remember Marc Bolan?
I bet you thought 'a dishy catch'.
When he wore his silver jacket
and silver eyeshadow to match.

Do you recall the Osmonds?
'Oh' how the girls did scream
When Donny sang his songs of love
He was every schoolgirls' dream.

And what about Gary Glitter
Who wore the most outrageous suits
of silver, gold and sparkly bits
and great big whopping boots.

Then we had the Rollers
How I loved it when they sang
the songs like ''Bye Bye Baby'
and the famous 'Shangalang'.

Adam Ant was soon to follow
to fame he quickly rose.
In his dandy highwayman attire
and a stripe across his nose.

Now they're listening to the warbling
and dancing to the rave.
They're taking drugs like Ecstasy
which will send them to the grave

Half the groups they ought to shoot
and the drugs they ought to ban.
So I'll stick with songs like 'Puppy Love'
And stay an Osmonds fan

A J Hudson

CONSIDER

Consider yourself,
your actions,
the way people see you.

Flirt? No, sociable, but
that's all. Nothing more,
just fun.

Mad? No, just different, but
people are scared of the abnormal
and usually don't like it, what
is normal?
Just having fun.
Consider yourself,
calm down, don't go
over the top.
People don't like it,

Well,
I never did anything
to you.
I think you'll find I'm a
nice person.
So what's *your* problem?

Like it!

and it's no contest for popularity.

Sylvie Wright (15)

My Best Friend

I turned to speak but you're not there
All there is, is an empty chair
A well worn seat where you once sat
Arms threadbare, cushions still flat.

I miss that look within your eye
You'd turn away as if so shy
Then you'd look back, yes I'm still there
As you sat so proud in your old armchair.

Those winter nights seemed oh so long
I'd sit and play your favourite song
You'd sit in that chair day after day
Your face alight, like a golden sunray.

We'd walk through the park, by the river too
You by my side so loyal and true
Mile upon mile we would cover
I know in my heart there'll be no other.

Old age you know, I was told
I awoke one morning and found you cold
As stiff as a board, robbed of life
It reminds me so much of my darling wife.

But now you're gone, I sit and read
Pause for a moment, look up at your lead
It still hangs there, next to the door
I picture your tail drumming the floor.

A squeaky toy lies in your bed
The memories of you within my head
Ears pricked up, head held high
It's hard to believe you had to die.

David Carl Webster

SHERWOOD: CLUMBER PARK

The false lake and the careful view
from stone arched bridge to church
and through the rhododendron woodland
to the stable block,
(no horses now, but tea rooms,)
where the bosses kept their other slaves
in light and air above the earth;
the bedrock where
beneath the seams of human lives,
the veins of coal,
the children, wives worked out the day
as if in night.

The Great Oak,
hollow now and plastic,
heart injected, propped,
fantastic, tortured, unapproachable,
outstood the merry bands now gone
that stood against the Thatcher years,
King John and Butcher Hesletine.
And with them depth and dark
and nights where Robin would be singing out
a shaft to pierce your heart.

Terri Legrys

Morning Flash

I wake up in the morning
And everything seems bare,
What's this close to me?
And what's that over there?

The banging of the shutters
The creeping of the stair,
Why does everything around me
Seem so here and there?

But just in a few seconds
Everything's back, and right as rain,
The morning flash is over now
Just as quickly as it came.

Beth Simpson (13)

UNTITLED

Oh little tiny snowdrops
on the grass so green
When the snow is melting
your little heads are seen
They smell as sweet as any other
but not so sweet as my dear old mother.

Graham Bailey (7)

THE NIGHT

Trying to sleep within the darkness of the night,
weird noises sound much louder,
not the same as in daylight.

Ghostly feelings ever haunting, thoughts of devils,
demons, sprites, eerie shapes and dark filled corners,
shadows cast by tricks of light.

Wind starts howling, sounding fierce, creaking floorboards,
doors and stairs, the overpowering fear of darkness,
monsters creeping from their lairs.

Eyes won't close, they search the darkness, imaginations
run amok, eventually when sleep comes drifting,
the darkness is quite soon forgot.

Gill Whyman

WINTER IS NIGH . . .

Summer has almost gone, and the winter is creeping in.
The leaves are turning colour and the flowers and shrubs look grim.

Soon the leaves will be falling all upon the ground,
it'll look like a carpet in winter
colours of red, gold and brown.

The trees will all be naked and bare, except for the holly bush,
that'll have red berries on everywhere.

The ground will get hard and frosty, shrubs and trees will go to sleep,
including the old hedgehog he's tucked up under a heap.

It'll be hard for the wildlife if the snow hits the ground,
they'll have to work twice as hard to see what can be found.

We'll be seeing more of little robin,
he never fails to show,
his red chest stands out as he hops about in the snow.

The fox he will be calling in my garden too,
I'll make him very welcome, I already do.

I love all the wildlife and I'm ready to help them out,
even more if the snow lies about.

Jackie Ann Middleton

STOP AND THINK

Will we ever know the meaning of within,
When all we see is without;
Will we ever trust our troubled lives,
When all we are taught is doubt;
Will we ever be portrayed as good,
When all we see is sin;
Will we ever love our neighbour
As we do our next of kin;
Will we take the time to colour our dreams
Or just leave them black and white;
When will we pick ourselves up
And try to see the light;
Will we ever take a thirsty child's cup
And pour them out a drink;
Was this poem just a waste of time, or
Has it made you stop and *think?*

Catherine R Taylor (16)

MIND MATTERS

What awesome sounds crack the quiet of the night
With flesh roughcast and face a Persilled white,
I struggle with an over-clouded sleep-washed mind
To unriddle, to unearth that thunder kind.

From the snugness of a bed hoodwinked in sleep
I scramble forth with jelly feet and logic in a heap
To hunt this wrecker spirit of the spooky sphere
But am unfit to rationalise if it is near.

The din twangs on with tumultuous spite
While I become helpless in the uneven fight
No one to muzzle this cuckooed ghoul
Only one senseless chicken-hearted fool.

I long to end the distressing labour
and conceive, only God would grant this favour.
I entreat my lord, my heavenly Maker
To deliver me from this silence-breaker.

Margaret Kelly

GRATITUDE

In the silence of the morning
at the dawn of a new day
I often let my thoughts fly
over the hills and far away
To the old farmstead
nestling 'neath the hills
where in the springtime
I'd gather daffodils
Run home to mother's cooking -
She was a super cook
always good, plain cooking -
without a cookery book

Nothing too much trouble
she'd listen to my woes
In the winter I huddled by the fire
warming my poor toes
We had no central heating
only oil lamps
But the warmth from mother's kitchen
made up for cold and damp

So many different memories
go racing through my head
Lying 'neath the duvet in my nice warm bed
Listening to the breathing of my beloved spouse
The central heating belching out its warmth
around the house
I appreciate the comforts of this
modern time
Values may be different -
But the living is sublime

Myrtle Wright

Sir Paul McCartney

Pleasant Mature,
Passive Modest,
Peaceful Muses,
Popular Man.
Produces Marvellous,
Perfect Melodies,
Passionate Magnificent.
Pop Music.
Prolific Master,
Positive Mind,
Poetic Magician,
Sir Paul McCartney!

Jon Perigud

The Biter Gets Bitten!

Mealtimes when Tele-Sales call - all inspired,
'No thanks, double glazing and porch not required,'
'Flyers' that fall out of newspapers, quite hidden,
or post asking for charities - 'already given'.
Nor would I win another 'free' holiday cruising the 'Med',
have been, got the tee shirt, cost an arm and a leg!
My resistance to sales talk is normally quite high,
but husband has always been a bit 'pie in the sky'

So I'll keep an eye on the money; whilst watching out for him,
but I can't resist the Lottery - who knows, we could win!

Dorothy Brookes

EARTH'S ENDING

Earth's shrivelled lungs, pocket
by pocket,
Felled,
Fired,
Wasted.

Each fume-filled gasp
Clogs
Chokes
Constricts airways.

At bay, the rains signal
Remission,
Respite
Reprieve.

Brief hope.

Therapy soothes the maiming frenzy.
The global village traversing like the
Lymphatic system
Multiplies
Migrates
Deadly infection.

Across a landscape still echoing past beauty.

S A Ladbrooke

FAME

'You can write a poem'
That's what my husband said
'I know that you can do it
Standing on your head!'
Well everyone in this life
No matter what their name
Has fifteen minutes so they say
To earn they're bit of fame
I can't remember who it was that
Gave that little quote
But you can bet your bottom dollar
It wasn't for what he wrote!
No matter how I tried though,
No words of inspiration
The only thing that led me on
Was that old sin 'temptation'?
Oh well at least I tried love,
Yes, I really did
And we would have had such fun
Spending that hundred quid!

Lorraine Saunders

Folly Of War

Is mankind mad that he permits
This shedding of human wine?
Does he forget this life of ours
Was the gift of the Lord Divine?
And yet, throughout this world today
We see no love. Instead
By man's own hand the virgin soil
Is spoilt by wasted dead.

This earth should be a happy place,
Where men can work and play,
But no! Through jealousy and greed
We all turn out to slay.
Perhaps one day we'll see our wrongs
But dearly has it cost.
We'll turn to God and follow him
And find what we have lost.

Leslie J Watkins

TINTERN

(Written at Tintern Abbey, early morning March 2nd 1990)

Misty ships upon the Wye, they turn and look,
then pass me by.
Pinnacles towering in the frosty air, looking
windward, stark and bare.
Looming Tintern, ages gone, every brick
the poet's charm.
Ghostly ships of a bygone day, caught in time.
Left to decay

Elizabeth Knight

UNTITLED

'I love you'
I hear you say,
but please can you tell me
in which way?

Is it as a friend, or a little bit more?
I simply need to know,
as I think I should tell you
I love you also.

Do you know
You mean the world to me,
As you are the only one
That has set my heart free.

So when you decide
which way to go
please don't forget
to let me know!

Alison Billingham

O

In a blink of an eye they were gone . . .
Gone.
Gone, never to return to those they loved.
Whilst the perpetrators of this bloody carnage have returned . . .
Home.
And are able to continue feathering their cosy nests.

So we blink our eyes. Yet they still remain . . .

Janice Rose

My Dad

A dad is head of the family a father and a friend
Someone who is always there and on whom you can depend
So thanks for all you have done Dad and for seeing me through
I hope I can be like you Dad - and pattern my life on you.

Times have not always been easy - but you were always there
To listen and to understand and let me know you cared
A friend in times of trouble that's what you have been to me
I hope I can be like you Dad when I have a family.

I know one day you will leave me and when it is time to go.
Please God that I can be strong Dad - as you have made me so
But I shall miss you so much Dad - and shed many a silent tear.
In the silence I will remember that you will always be near

I will try to keep on going Dad but it will be hard to do.
I know for the rest of my life Dad
My thanks will go out to you.

Marjorie Ridley

END OF A CENTURY

End of a century is nearly here
Oh! What will the new one endure
Countries who suffer from famine and drought
No more should they be without.

Over the years machinery has taken mans jobs
Some for better some for worse
But all the pollution we all curse
Will the new century be on a better course.

L J Male

Homage

My honeymoon was spent at Bonn,
I stood and gazed with pensive thoughts;
I stood and looked with reverency,
And marvelled at our human thoughts.

Oh tell me not that mournful tale
Of German souls that are unwell;
Oh tell me not to hate this race,
For greatness vibrates in this place.

I walked along the flowing Rhine,
Where he himself so often walked;
A place of beauty and, it seemed
A dead man followed me unseen.

I saw the room where he was born;
I walked the streets where he had played;
I stood and looked with reverency;
True greatness lives beyond the grave.

Beyond the grave the trumpets sound;
Beyond the grave the cymbals crash;
Beyond the grave his thoughts still live,
Such greatness never fades away.

When all our hatreds, vanities and jests
Are superseded by the realms of death,
'Tis then too late our follies to perceive,
For we are dead and therefore cannot heed
The moral that the hand of nature shows
To all mankind, but still we do not know the way
To live, and yet we all must die.

C F Herniman

In The Red

If we could revert to the older ideals
of paying as you went along
Society today would be a lot better
there'd be a lot less that was wrong

It's all very easy to run up a bill
with the plastic that's freely in use
Before you realise what you have done
you're putting your head in the noose

There comes a point when it loses its value
and you're spending way over the top
But once you have started this social disease
it's very much harder to stop

When receiving a letter much to your surprise
you're given a higher limit
So it starts again the same routine
by now you're really stuck in it

It's at this conjuncture you're told to pay up
they've given you 30 days
No problem, no panic, you know what to do
it can be solved in so many ways

A bank loan's the answer pay back in one go
consolidate all your arrears
Taken straight from your wages, it's not really missed
you can pay it back over five years

This done quite promptly, the company decide
you're quite a good risk for them
Another card arrives, extending your credit
and it starts all over again

The problem arises when the bank says no more
you're up to your eyes so it seems
The company are asking for immediate payment
but you're living beyond your means

So what do you do to get out of this fix
do you resort to crime
Take the chance, but it doesn't work
and now you've got plenty of time

Ian Pearch

THE CRICKET MATCH

Sitting at the cricket
On a sunny afternoon,
All is set and ready
Hope they get going soon.

Bowling a maiden over
But not the two-legged kind,
Oh no, that's such a pity
He's just got caught behind.

First slip and long leg
It all adds to the fun,
That is such a smashing shot
He doesn't need to run.

Four runs, or perhaps six
Lost the ball, in a fix,
Get another, start again
Now, here comes a shower of rain.

Quickly get the covers on
Just a storm we hope,
Children running everywhere
They do not stand and mope.

Now the sun is coming out
The game gets going again,
Lots of shouts and cheers go up
As we strive to win, in vain.

Winifred Shore

CORNWALL

Cornwall, beloved Cornwall,
Dear county I adore,
The hills, the dales, the rock-strewn moors,
That stretch from shore to shore.
You are an inspiration, to people everywhere,
The beauty of your countryside
Is rich beyond compare.

The heather and the moorland,
The gorse and bracken too,
The tips of china-clay waste,
Reach up to skies of blue.
The treacherous rocks we notice,
As on the cliffs we roam,
All go to give you, Cornwall
A character all your own.

And so beloved Cornwall
From Tamar to Lands End,
With voices raised, in thankful praise
Our lives in you we spend.
And when the sun is setting
Deep and glorious in the west,
We who love you Cornwall,
Are sure you are the best.

Sue Stanaway

Ariadne On Naxos

Time goes and comes in its blue loops.
The loops would make a fine quilt, but I cannot hold them.
I am naked; nothing touches me.
Before, my feet were strong and nimble;
my hands had eyes and ears, and for my beloved
they spun the tale of his triumph and freedom.
Now the sun is my father, my mother is the sea,
the night my velvet bed,
but where, where is my love?
In vain I try to catch the gossamer threads
trailing still from the golden day he left me,
his black silken sails dipping, slipping
into the rose-pink void.

Frances Thompson

TOPSHAM

I'd choose no other place but this
Old sailors' synthesis
Of sea and salt and home

Here water slides the years away:
Hulks and quays decay
But the past remains

And twilight conjures up the days
Of vanished ships, forgotten ways
And the sound of birds . . .

Once rang the streets with laughter
And every poor man's daughter
Loved a handsome sailor.

Driftwood on distant shores their ships
Are now, and over all their kissing lips
The green grass grows.

Whose footsteps echo in the street?
Who stands where strand and water meet?
The moon replies:

'See all along the living river
The water stirring, reeds a-quiver:
Their ghosts return.

I saw them born:
They will not go until the dawn
Comes slowly back.'

I look again, but at my side
Is only starlight
And the surging tide.

Tim Williams

SUNDAYS

Petherton girls are squat and square
with slatey eyes and a sleepy stare
that have a strange and sultry air
of sturdy joys -
on Sundays.

Ponderous foot on foot they climb
Ham Hill, hand-holding. Church bells chime.
In Somerset there's always time
for Petherton boys -
on Sundays . . .

Sheila Glen Bishop

WORDS

'Words' they tell us of life's pleasure,
'Words' are something we should treasure.
When we are far apart
They are kept deep in our heart.
Those three words that are so true
That beautiful saying
'I love you'.

Andrew Johnson

St Matthew

The peaceful figure,
Sat on a stool,
Quiet as a dream,
No one to disturb him,

The peaceful figure,
Of St Matthew,
In his crumpled robes,
With his bare feet rested on a book,

The peaceful figure,
Surrounded by the trees and hills,
He concentrates so hard,
The peaceful, tired, figure.

Jenny Masters (14)

Grey Picture

An artist's palette with a trace
Of whites, yellows, browns and blacks;
Holds the key to the human race
And everything it lacks.
Cultures are hard to tolerate;
Tongues not well understood,
But man his own problems create
And would solve them if he could!

Colours are the criteria
Whether etched black, white or yellow
Whichever hue may be near
If different - you despise the fellow.
Mix a pot with all the tones,
Let evolution paint the page;
That painter would dress his bones
With the acceptable colour beige!

If everyone was drawn the same,
Perhaps the rest would follow,
Happiness could be the aim -
An end to all life's sorrow.
But man will never be at peace,
There's much too much to contemplate.
It is the nature of the beast
To leave too much to fate.

So in the end, the artist's brush
Would style another hell
Man will always headlong rush
And sketch his own death-knell.

Susan Naile

BLACK LINES

Looking through my address book
Turning pages to see
Black lines
Crossed names
Memories

More gone now than are left
So many names etched away
Black lines
Crossed names
Come what may

Checking my Christmas card list
How many have I got to send?
Black lines
Crossed names
Absent friends

Damon Naile

Physical

In lit renewed warehouses
on wharves of the docks
wistful wives are seated and working-out.

Pulling pushing the blocks
to fill loveless evenings
gone seven o'clock.

All the menfolk
have ambled the shortest road
to their nearest watering-hole.

Amid smoke and noise his bar stool will creak
as he sways and rocks,
he becomes fatter, heavier.

Her skin will be wet her apparatus will creak
when she moves the blocks,
but will be fitter, healthier.

And should he return
and verbally impugn
before knocking her around the bedroom,

she will have the strength
to lift infant, carry-cot
and brimming case to another place.

S J Wright

TALE OF THREE TOWNS

What remains of the old three towns
it could be said would best be found
in the human remnants one may meet
in the doorways of the union streets.
Travelling time and hardly noticed
like the wraiths that linger from
the backroom seances,
more like ghosts in their camouflage coats
they blend with the daytime scenery
and dream and dream and dream . . .
of the cafes and theatres and tailors
and bars . . . and the 'gentlemen only' clubs.

Michael Sharron Palmer

An Englishman's Home

When the visitors are all gone
What joy
To rumple up the cushions
Leave the crumbs
Upon the dining table
And withdraw
To flick our ash upon the
ancestral hearth!

When the visitors are all gone
What fun
To read the calf-bound volumes
Rock upon
The antique rocking-chair
And ignore
The warning, 'Do not touch
this harpsichord'!

When the visitors are all gone
What chance
To find ourselves, alone
With all these *things!*
For then we must be quiet
And discover
Why they - and we - are
gathered here together.

Joan Kirby

HOUGHTON STREET

Walking through Houghton Street,
perception films in black and white
apocalyptic buildings watching
from either side
as I stride
anonymous through its cast
and say my part in its silent movies.
Walking through the library
walking through everyone,
four crypts with desks
and chairs for the living,
haunt the knowledge
borrowed by others
and escape unnoticed,
my only points of reference.

Andrew A Logan

My Sons

My comfort when I'm sad
My love when I'm cross

My reality
in stress

Our love is entire

To take all
and give all

My help
My cuddles
My sons

L Fusciardi

POSTCARD VIEW OF NEWHAVEN

Harbour View

The army of seagulls dive-bomb the
water as the ferries move on.
Gold-coloured fish lie, as if sunbathing
on the fishing boats.
All night, light look-like wiggle lines
rolling along calm water.
The water sparkles in the moonlight.

Beach View

The divers splashing and splashing in
the water.
The children run, playing happy on the
sand.
Making castles in the sun.
Boats go in and out all day long.
People catching whitebait at high tide.

Market View

Groups of old ladies discussing what
to buy.
Talking about when next to meet.
Shouts of 'Buy my fish, they're very
fresh.'
Cries of market people and mumbling
of people talking.
A wonderful town.

Jade Fitch

Endurance Test

Gathered light of days long past,
Fragmented moments that are lost.
Memories of once that was,
Half captured in the now that is.
Where is it all? Where has it gone?
Merciful time? Relentless time?
Will all be remembered of days gone by?
Will it all screen before my heart?
Whose cloak will shield the agony?
Or will I find, to my relief,
That merciful time has paid the score
And power has gone from days gone by?
To resurrect one shining hour
Of long dead moments of delight
Or tortured moments of despair.

Kay Bailes

The Way We Are

The way we are
Shapes what we do
What we do depends upon
Circumstances, opportunity
and
being.
Being there at the right time.
Doing.
Doing the right thing at the
right time.
How we are depends upon the
doing of the right thing
at the right time
being there
just *being*, being ourselves.

Su McKenzie

February Fomentations

We leave the warmth of the house with supreme reluctance,
Fortified by porridge and steaming green tea
and bending against the cruel east wind,
'That wind would cut the eye out of you'. My mother used to say
'That wind' blows through the seemingly bare branches,
On closer inspection they sport tight buds of new growth
Anxious for a shaft of watery sunshine to coax them into a spirit of renewal.

My eyes water and droplets course down my frozen cheeks,
The calluses on my blood-letting hand stick to my thermal gloves
I endeavour to press my fingertips into my palms
In a frenzied effort to regain some sensation,
My daughter asks: 'Why are you crying?'
I try to answer but numb cheeks prevent a reply
Other than that of a stumbling inebriate,
I struggle to turn the key in the lock
Press the switch on the kettle, peel my gloves off
and introduce my frozen digits to water gushing from the hot tap;
The postman has delivered a holiday brochure
I close my eyes as my cold lips make contact with a
comforting drink.
Delicious reflections of balmy breezes caressing my body
Invigorating my slowly defrosting frame.

Gabrielle Whyte

Dead On Time

Two twenty:

Not that door.
That's the exit.
The way in is round the corner.
Death is a one-way system.

Round the corner
We meet
Grey smiles on grey faces,
Whispering grey platitudes.

Two twenty-six:

Recessional electronic strains
Labour through the heavy doors,
Declaring the departure
Of those who went before.

Our silent hearse relinquishes
Its sleeping cargo.

Two thirty:

Our friend, in overcoat of oak,
A single rose upon the wooden chest,
Shouldered by black shuffling feet,
We take our turn upon that cold conveyor.

For twenty-two minutes
We are permitted
To ease into our sorrow,
Contemplate our grief.
Twenty-two minutes
In which to reflect upon
Ninety-four extraordinary years.

Two fifty-six:

The laboured dirge resurges.
Curtains unlatched,
Our friend dispatched,
Dead on time.

Stella Redman

Look And Live

Live not for tomorrow or that which is past,
Look not to the future or things that won't last,
Look only at the present and what we can do,
For those all around us whose blessings are few.

Live not for tomorrow and yesterdays gone,
Look not to the future for it won't be long,
Look only to the present and how we can ease
The suffering around us, dear Lord, help us please.

Live not for tomorrow nor yearn for things done,
Look not at the raindrops and long for the sun,
Look only at now and be happy therein
Be grateful for the mercies that free us from sin.

Live not for tomorrow and let yesterday go,
Look on not in anger, pride, envy or woe
Look for the goodness that's in every day,
And thank God Almighty that he's led us this way.

M Stoneham

The Ballad Of Dan Foley

Dan Foley was a collier,
From that distant emerald isle,
Generations of his kin,
Had hewed the hard black pile.

With blue scarred hands,
And muscles that had worn,
He wheeled a pick, sure and quick,
To earn some precious corn.

Foley loved this life,
Of that you could be sure,
Swallowing clouds of dust,
He had to find a cure.

So he took his medicine,
He drank jugs of beer,
Inside the local ale-house,
Frequently, throughout the year.

Standing in the lamp-lit bar,
His vocal chords he used,
And patrons of The Lion pub,
All were quite amused.

Working at Barrs Bank pit,
The miner met his fate,
A pit-prop gave, there was a fall,
And he stood at Heaven's gate.

A flustered St Peter said,
'Daniel Foley you are late,
Please go back, my son,
Then choose another date.'

So when some still, winter's night,
In mid-stride, you suddenly hear,
A strong Celtic singing voice,
Then Foley's ghost, is near!

Alan Dawes

TRUE FRIENDSHIP

The strings stretch far across the world,
Invisible to naked eye,
Yet bonds forged truly never break
In everlasting friendship.

No matter what life has in store,
The sharing of the good and bad,
Can lessen burdens and bring joy
To everlasting friendship.

As we progress through life's array,
Of happenings, meetings, foes and friends,
It is with heartfelt thanks we seek
For everlasting friendship.

The power is there though distance far,
The closeness, empathy and love,
Will stand the test of time in strength
Through everlasting friendship.

Pauline Bunkin

SHATTERED

Shattered
Like glass
A ghost from my past
Brought back memories of you
You left me
Shattered
Like glass
And no matter how much
Time will pass
I'm still shattered
Like glass

Louise Janet Tweedie

Eagle and Child

There is a cottage at the top of the bank
From the Rose and Crown about a mile
Not very far from the Youth Hostel
It is called the Eagle and Child.

Now this old cottage has a legend
That one day an eagle flew by
A baby on the ground it did befriend
Then took the baby high in the sky.

When the bird finally got to its nest
He carefully placed it within
He put his own birds to the test
To be brought up with his own kith and kin.

There are some lovely views from there
You can see back forest and the roaches
You can just imagine many years ago
When people travelled round with horse and coaches.

Wherever you go you will not find
Such beautiful hills and dales
Where the people you meet are kind
And will tell you many tales.

May Ward

HORACE

You hear the nurses call your name
As you zoom around with your Zimmer frame.
You look for things upon the floor
And try to find some hidden door.
Then you sit beside your bed,
Voices talking in your head.
You talk to people from the past,
Your memory is fading fast.
You eat your food just like a child,
Once you were young and strong and wild.
Horace, this should never be,
You should be left with dignity.

K Fallon

Paws For Thought

They're awfully good to me really,
As I only do things when I wish;
There is always fresh food in my dish.
They're awfully good to me really,
They pay frequent veterinary bills
For prevention and cure of ills.
They're awfully good to me really,
They don't seem to mind me leaving hairs
Scattered around on carpets and chairs.
They're awfully good to me really,
When I scratch and infrequently spray
They accept it as being my way.
They're awfully good to me really,
When sometimes I bring them a dead bird
Expressions of thanks are to be heard.
They're awfully good to me really,
If I don't want to 'go' in cold ground,
Freshly cleaned litter trays are around.
They're awfully good to me really,
I can come and can go through a door
All it needs is a push with a paw.
They're awfully good to me really,
And there's always a welcoming lap
When I fancy a stroke and a nap.
They're awfully good to me really,
I get my own way, day after day
If I purr and appear to say -
'They're awfully good to me really.'

S R Ramsden

RELAXING MOMENTS

I love to stand upon the bridge
And watch the flowing river
And see the trout swim in and out
Their bodies all a-quiver

The ducks come swimming up to you
To see if you have brought
Some dainty bits to supplement
The food which they have caught

So soon they gobble up the food
And then away they go
To wait awhile, till someone else
To them some food will throw.

Mary M Collis

JERRY

I little thought, when first I took him in
How much the tabby cat would mean to me.
A favour for a friend, 'Yes, I'll look after him.'
And so he came, and never went away.
A large and bumbling cat with liquid eyes.

Despite his age, he soon became
Accustomed to my ways.
We grew together, tolerant and loved.
And though he would complain
If I was late with food, or coming home,
He knew I would return, would be there just for him.

He had endearing traits -
Of patting my grey hairs,
Of holding up his paw, beseeching love,
Or asking for his share - the only time
He drank his milk, when we sat down at four.

His eyes grew dim,
But still he seemed to cope,
Though never roaming far,
Content to stay in some warm spot
In my small garden plot.

His favourite place.
Flower-strewn, rain blessed.
He sleeps there now,
Sun-warmed, at rest.

Cynthia M Manning

Across The Miles

Winging through the letterbox
A letter came today
Airmailed from New Zealand,
That's half a world away.
Opening it with eager hands
We really couldn't wait
To read the news of those we love
We didn't hesitate.
To know they're all so happy,
That good health came as well,
To read their loving greetings
Meant more than words can tell.
Although they're far away from us,
Our letters seem to show
That we are all so near in heart
No matter where we go.
That distance is no barrier
When there, between the miles,
The love that flies on golden wings
Returns, to give us smiles.
And so we send our dearest love
'God keep them safe', we pray
And may we be together soon
O happy happy day.

Enid Rathbone

THE STAG

Concealed in the deep, dark wood he stands,
The majestic stag, several hands high,
Full antlers glistening, still and quiet, always listening,
Ready to run at the slightest sound, of thundering hooves or baying hounds,
Suddenly he pricks up his ears, the distant hunt is what he hears,
No time to lose, through the wood he flies, into the field, under blue skies,
Off he runs, ahead of the chase, he can hear the hounds, he must win the race.

Loud thundering hooves, as the horses dash,
Coats of red like a fiery flash,
Close behind now, he feels the hounds' breath,
He must go faster or risk death.
Suddenly the river, near, with a terrible splash he forgets his fear,
Swimming hard he reaches the bank,
Exhausted he stops and then looks back,
No sign of the hunt, just the water he hears,
Today he'll not die, his head he rears,
Off into the wood so quiet he will stay,
Recovered to run another day.

June Light

Nostalgia

Plant for me
In memory
A rowan tree
Of mountainside
And valley wide
By gushing rill

It stands, until
In autumn
Red and yellow berries
Hang along its branches
Colours bright

On misty days
We walk the stony ways
And rest
Beside its solitary stance
Knowing, at a glance
Its place is here.

Constance Wateridge

A Love-Like Poem

Oh God, I wish that you were with me now,
To hold and comfort me, and then to vow
Our love will last until our lives run out,
To take away my loneliness and doubt.
Without you I am lost, alone, forlorn,
An embryo still waiting to be born,
Whose birth occurs each time you reappear,
To take away my doubts and ease my fear
Of losing the one love I've ever known
And make me feel I'll never be alone.

If there was some way I could ease this pain
If only you would come to me again.
Do you love me like this? Can it be true?
Or are you even now with someone new?
Oh please, please come, I need you so tonight
For solitude is darkness, you are light.
My heart aches so for you that it will break
Come, please come to me and take
Me in your arms and hold me evermore
Then I will know just what I'm living for.

Naufer Mohamed Salim

Worlds Apart

As they cower in a small tin hut,
I watch.
As they cry out in fear,
I watch.
A single child's shoe in a ghost town,
a shrill cry in the night.
A bloodstained toy on the deserted ground,
Then I turn off the television
and settle down for the night.

Gemma Louise Cole

THE GATE

I am the gate at which we met
I am the look which we exchanged
I am the shy smile which you gave
I am the thrill when our hands touched
I am the stars under which we stood
I'm the years we spent together
I am the love that we both shared
I am the despair when you died
I am the gate where it all began.

John J Allan

BEACH INVADERS

Upon the deep blue rippling sea streams shafts of sunbeams' rays.
Like a billion tiny diamonds in tumbling fountain sprays.
White foam floats on incoming tide by undercurrents below
And drifts onto golden sandy shores to disperse like melting snow.
The sightless winds not blowing yet encircling gulls glide high
Clouds are non-existent in the awning of the sky.
Expanse of coastline stretches twixt land that greets the sea
Sounds of lapping water's edge gives, background melody.
One gets a sense of timelessness such peaceful harmony
An ethereal feeling one may say a dream-like quality.
But invaders are coming to this beautiful coastal strip
By hordes with total disregard who'll leave a rubbish tip.

N Radford

THE FAIRYTALE ZENITH

Pools that shimmer fine in moonlight
Broken rainbows skip the skylight
Souls are swept along a tightrope
April springs are full of good hope
Angels never weep in silence
Always ask the Lord for guidance.

Trade our lives for lasting peace
And love that reaches 'neath our dreams
Dive in deep to rivers blue
And never will our hearts remain
Unable to beat true again.

Linking arms with saints and sinners
All unite may God forgive us
Spinning moonshells through my shadow
Darkened skies that cross my eyes
Yet whisper golden lullabies.

Dancing lightly through your breath
And longing for your sweet caress
Sing me sing me songs of joy
And bring me dreams that I can reach
So never lose my wishes wanting
Let us build a world of loving.

Daniel Cloute

WATER

A trickle of water,
Through the hand,
In the stream that runs,
Over the land.

Rippling and gurgling
As it goes
Through meadows and valleys,
Twisting and turning,
Ever wider - deeper.

Ducks glide in,
To feed and preen.

Fish dart and spawn
In the brook.
Quite unaware
of the fisherman,
With line and hook.

River runs on
To meet the sea,
There to find,
More mystery.

Eveline Nash Gaging

The Monster

Evil lurks
In the corner of the room
Waiting
Waiting to grab her
To ignore her screams
And pitiful cries
And to rob her of her innocence
As it has every night
For the past five years
It knows no mercy
It cannot be classed as a person
But as a monster
A dark, evil monster
That hides every night
In the same place
Her fear stirs no emotion
Inside its cruel heart
When will it stop?
Every night
She screams for a help
That never comes
But it is only a matter of time
Before the evil is uncovered
Only a matter of time
Before the help
She so desperately needs arrives
And only a matter of time
Before someone kills the monster.

Ali Forward-Preedy

A Summer's Day

The birdsongs wake me on this perfect day
I draw the curtains and survey my world
The sun shines warm from skies all blue not grey
The grass, dew-dappled, lies 'neath trees unfurled.

The trees stand tall and still - no breezes blow
The air feels light, as light as my glad heart
I skip through morning chores and feel a glow
Of pure and simple bliss to be a part

Of nature's bounty on this blesséd morn
For we are partners in an unspoiled span
Which arcs from dawn till dusk - and earth's reborn -
Such loving links 'twixt nature, God and man.

Jane Mortimer